Green Kids

Recycling

Neil Morris

QEB Publishing

Copyright © QEB Publishing, Inc. 2008

Published in the United States by
QEB Publishing, Inc.
23062 La Cadena Drive
Laguna Hills, CA 92653

www.qeb-publishing.com

Library of Congress Control Number: 2008010278

ISBN 978 1 59566 540 9

Printed and bound in China

Author Neil Morris
Consultant Bibi van der Zee
Editor Amanda Askew
Designer Elaine Wilkinson
Picture Researcher Maria Joannou
Illustrator Mark Turner for Beehive Illustration

Publisher Steve Evans
Creative Director Zeta Davies

Words in **bold** can be found in
the glossary on page 22.

Contents

That's garbage!

Garbage is made up of things that we throw away because we do not want them any more. It is also called waste. An empty drinks bottle is garbage because the drink has been drunk.

▶ *Many things, including plastic bottles, can be recycled rather than thrown away.*

Did you know?

In rich countries, each person throws away a sack of garbage every ten days—a village of 350 people would produce an elephant's weight in waste every week!

We throw all kinds of things away. Our waste includes paper and card, glass bottles, metals, and plastic. Kitchen and garden waste, and old clothes and rags are also thrown away.

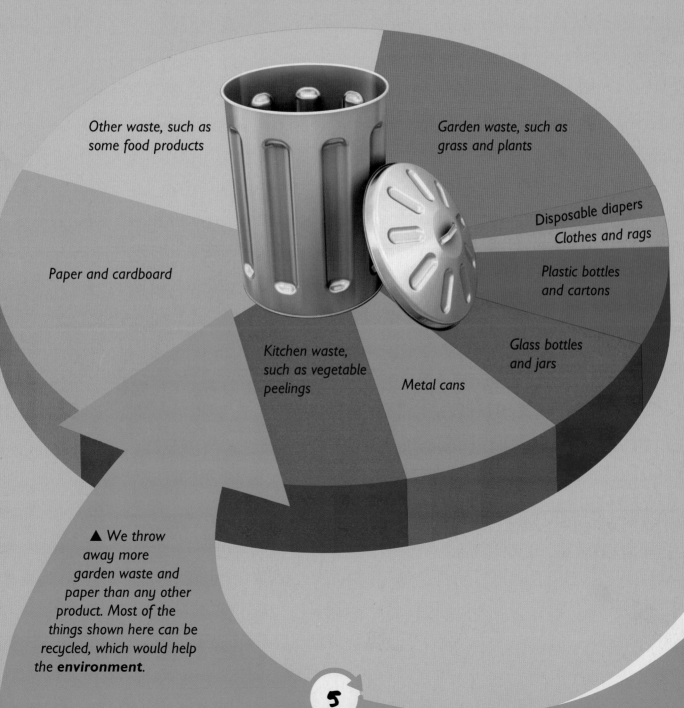

Other waste, such as some food products

Garden waste, such as grass and plants

Disposable diapers

Clothes and rags

Paper and cardboard

Plastic bottles and cartons

Glass bottles and jars

Kitchen waste, such as vegetable peelings

Metal cans

▲ We throw away more garden waste and paper than any other product. Most of the things shown here can be recycled, which would help the **environment**.

What happens to our waste?

General waste goes into bins and these are emptied into special trucks. The trucks collect garbage from homes and schools.

◀ *Garbage trucks have machinery inside that crushes waste to make it smaller.*

Garbage trucks take most waste to **landfill sites**. There, the waste is tipped into a big hole in the ground. When the hole is full, the waste is buried.

▶ *This landfill waste will eventually be covered with dirt. The land may then be used as a country park or a golf course.*

Did you know?

The waste that is put into landfill sites in one minute would fill 15 buses.

▶ Before waste is put into an **incinerator** and burned, large claws turn it over to dry it.

Some of our waste is burned in large furnaces, which are hot ovens called incinerators.

The three Rs

We can help to produce less waste by putting the three Rs into action. The letters stand for **reduce**, **reuse**, and **recycle**.

Reducing means cutting down on waste by using less in the first place. For example, we could use less **packaging**. Some foods are wrapped in plastic, but instead we could buy them without the packaging.

▶ These apples are on a tray and wrapped in plastic. They could be bought loose to reduce waste.

You can do it

Start a "swap shop" with your friends. Bring toys or books that you no longer use or need. Friends might like to swap them for something you want.

We can use things again instead of throwing them away. You could use a shoebox to store special toys or drawings.

▶ Instead of being thrown away or recycled, a jam jar can be reused as a pen or pencil holder.

Don't throw it away

When we throw things away, we waste the **materials** they are made from. It is better to recycle. Recycling makes a new product out of something that has been used before.

▲ *Empty plastic bottles and other containers can be recycled to make new ones.*

When you go shopping, you can buy goods that have been recycled. Look out for the symbols or words that tell you notepads, tissues, or toilet paper are made of recycled paper.

You can do it

You could sort garbage at home into groups, such as paper and cardboard, glass, metal, and plastic. Find out where you can take the garbage or when it is collected.

New paper for old

Trees are turned into **pulp**, which is then used to make paper. It takes a lot of energy to turn wood into paper. We can save trees and energy by using pulp from recycled paper.

▶ Trees are mashed into pulp, which will be used to make large sheets of paper. The sheets will then be cut to smaller sizes.

Did you know?

Making one ton of recycled paper saves 17 trees. This makes 700 phone books and saves enough energy to heat your home for a year.

When paper from books and newspapers is recycled, the ink must be removed. Soap is added to the pulp to wash the ink away. Some recycled paper is not as bright white as nonrecycled paper.

Recycled paper

▲ *Normally, recycled paper is not **bleached**, so it may not be as white as bleached paper. This saves more energy and **chemicals**.*

Nonrecycled paper

Saving glass

Glass bottles and jars can be recycled many times. At the recycling plant, they are crushed. Then the glass is heated, so that it melts and can be shaped into new bottles.

You can do it

Keep a chart of the glass bottles you recycle. Recycling one glass bottle saves enough energy to power ten energy-saving light bulbs for an hour.

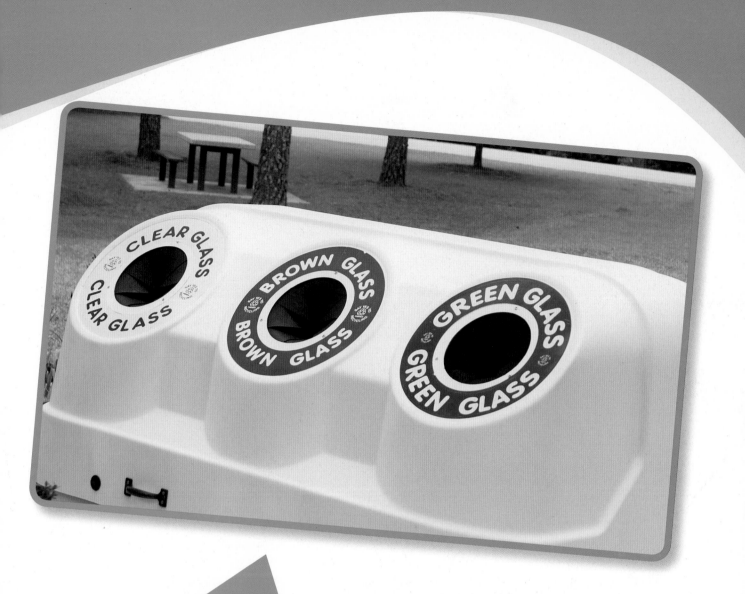

There are three bottle banks for different-colored glass. The colors—green, brown, and clear—are separated because if they were mixed, the recycled bottles would be a dull, muddy color.

▲ Bottle banks can be found in many places, including supermarkets, country parks, and on main streets.

Different metals

Cans can be recycled, too. Most drinks cans are made of **aluminum** and food cans are **steel**. The cans are separated when they are recycled so the different metals do not mix together.

Steel food can

Aluminum drinks can

▲ Cans should be washed out before they are recycled. Food cans should also have their labels removed.

There is a simple way to tell steel from aluminum. Hold a magnet against the can. If the magnet sticks to the can, it is probably made of steel. Aluminum is not magnetic.

Old metal cans are made into new ones in the same way as glass. The cans are crushed, melted, and reshaped.

◀ *These drinks cans have been crushed together, ready to be melted down to make new cans.*

You can do it

Have an empty drinks can drive at school—see how many you can collect. Recycling one can saves enough energy to run a television for three hours.

Plastic problems

Plastic is a strong, light material made from oil. The world is running out of oil, so we need to recycle as much plastic as possible, or use other materials.

▶ *Most bottled water comes in plastic bottles.*

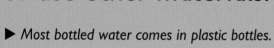

Did you know?

It takes three times more energy to make a new plastic bottle than a recycled one. Recycling one bottle saves enough energy to power a light bulb for six hours.

We can all help the environment by using fewer plastic bags. Materials that last a long time, such as fabric, are much better. Keep any plastic bags you are given, so that you can reuse them.

▲ *Fabric bags or reusable bags made from recycled materials are better for the environment. Many supermarkets now provide them.*

Green waste

Green waste comes from plants. It includes grass and leaves from the garden. Some green waste is made up of food leftovers, such as fruit and vegetable scraps.

▶ *In the fall, leaves fall off the trees. They can be raked up and put in special green waste or compost can.*

Did you know?

Every year, each person throws away 1,000 pounds of green waste—the same as 850 banana skins. In landfill sites, green waste produces methane gas, which is very smelly!

Green waste can be recycled at home by making a compost heap or putting it into a compost bin.

▼ Garden waste can be collected in a compost can. It takes at least six months for the compost to be made.

▲ Compost looks like crumbly soil. It is made from green waste.

Over several months, the plants rot, making a crumbly material called compost. Gardeners use compost to grow new plants in because it is full of goodness.

Glossary

aluminum	a non-magnetic, silvery metal
bleached	whitened by using chemicals
chemical	a substance made by mixing other substances together
environment	the world around us
incinerator	a large furnace (very hot oven) for burning waste
landfill site	a big hole in the ground, where waste is buried
material	a substance used to make things
packaging	the container that something is put in
pulp	a soft, wet mass
recycle	to make something new out of a thing that has been used before
reduce	to make the amount of something smaller
reuse	to use something again
steel	a strong metal made of iron and carbon

Index

Notes for parents and teachers

- Safety. Children should not handle garbage directly. They should always wear gloves and use litter-pickers. Do not touch anything you are unsure of. Be particularly careful with glass. Bottles may be cracked or chipped, so must be handled carefully.

- Go to a supermarket and look at all the things that could be recycled, especially packaging. Discuss why packaging is used (making items, such as food, look attractive). In some countries, shoppers can give packaging straight back to the store at the till point. Come up with other ideas to cut down on packaging.

- Think of other ways to reuse and recycle household items. Paper printed or written on one side can be cut up to the same size and stapled together to make a notepad. Christmas and birthday cards can be cut up and folded to make mini-cards or gift tags. Old socks can make glove puppets. Do you have any other ideas?

- Use newspaper pulp to make papier mâché. First, tear sheets of old newspaper into thin strips. Then tear the strips into small squares. Soak the newspaper pieces in warm water. When the paper is soft, rub it between your fingers until it is pulpy. Then squeeze out the water. Mix wallpaper paste, PVA glue, or flour with a little water and add to the pulp until the mixture is like sticky pastry. Then you can use the pulp for modeling. It could cover an old container and then a child could paint it.

- Another way of turning kitchen waste into compost and concentrated liquid plant feed is by using a wormery. This uses the natural action of worms and is guaranteed to be popular with children.

- Take children to see their local paper and bottle banks. Help them to post some items.

- Look through the book and talk about the pictures. Read the captions and then ask questions about other things in the photographs that have not been mentioned.